jB   Rubin, Susan
SALOMON   Goldman.

            Haym Salomon.

$16.95

DATE			

HAYM SALOMON
★ American Patriot ★

By Susan Goldman Rubin ★ Illustrated by David Slonim

Abrams Books for Young Readers
New York

The newspaper headlines declared the shocking news:

General George Washington losing to the British Redcoats!

"Army greatly distressed," said an article in the *New-York Gazette and the Weekly Mercury*. The troops have no meat, one of Washington's officers reported in the paper. "Many eat their shoes, shot pouches, etc. . . ." They need food, blankets, uniforms, and boots. Even their horses are hungry. "No men ever went through more or greater hardships . . . However we are *Americans* and *American Soldiers*."

In January 1776, Haym Salomon sat reading the *New-York Gazette* in his house on Broad Street.

How can I help? He wondered.

I am only a Jewish immigrant.

Haym had just come to America from Poland. Although he missed his family and friends, he wanted more than anything to live in a free country.

As a young man, Haym had traveled throughout Europe working in banks. He learned how to count money, save money, and loan money. He knew the price of silver and gold and understood what money from many other countries was worth. For instance, he could exchange German marks for Russian rubles, or Polish goldens for French francs. Along the way, he learned many languages—French, German, Russian, Italian, and English. And of course he knew Hebrew and Polish.

Now in New York, he put his knowledge to good use.

In those days, colonists used English pounds and shillings as well as American paper dollars and pennies. Immigrants also brought money from their native countries and kept using it in America. Haym was able to exchange or loan money for everyone. He was able to talk with his immigrant customers in their own languages. People found him to be honest and fair. They liked his good manners and gentle way of speaking.

At this time, the thirteen American colonies belonged to the British Empire.

However, King George III of England did not treat the colonists well. He forced Americans to pay extra money, called taxes, for ordinary things like newspapers, playing cards, and tea. So the colonists declared war on England, saying they wanted to be free and rule their own country. Among the many people who wanted change was Haym.

One day, someone knocked on Haym's door. It was his friend Alexander MacDougall.

"I'm leading a group called the Sons of Liberty," said Alexander. "We secretly fight the English. A couple of years ago, when an English ship arrived here in New York, we dressed up as Indians and dumped the cargo of tea overboard."

Haym sat forward and listened.

"Do you want to join us?" said Alexander. "I must warn you, it will be dangerous. Once, the British caught me for printing pamphlets and threw me in jail."

Haym thought carefully. He certainly did not want to get into trouble. On the other hand, he loved his new country. He had come all this way to find freedom.

"Yes," Haym told Alexander. "I will join your group. What do you want me to do?"

In June 1776, Haym closed his profitable business. He left New York with a wagon full of supplies for the American army. Haym rode many miles to Fort Ticonderoga at Lake George, New York. There he set up a tent to house coats, shoes, boots, blankets, and other things the soldiers needed badly and had no other way of getting. Every month, Haym paid a fee for the right to sell these goods from his tent. That money went to a fund for widows, orphans, and retired soldiers.

"Good work, Mr. Salomon," said General Philip Schuyler, the officer in command.

Haym had even brought eyeglasses packed in little wooden boxes tied with ribbons. "Try these on," he said to men who were having trouble reading. Local farmers also brought goods—meat, vegetables, and berries—to Haym's tent to sell to the soldiers.

In April of the following year, word came that the Redcoats, as the British soldiers were called, were going to attack New York City. General Washington and his troops were far north in Massachusetts and had to journey quickly to New York. As soon as Haym heard the news, he packed up and headed home to New York, too. By the time Haym arrived, the British had won the battle and had captured the city.

On September 20, 1776, in the middle of the night, a fire broke out.

Flames swept through the city. Smoke filled the air. By dawn, more than four hundred buildings had burned down.

British officers immediately suspected that the fire had been started by the Sons of Liberty. Rumors had spread that these patriots would rather see their city burn down than turn it over to the British.

"Let's get the Sons of Liberty!" cried the British. They rounded up the rebels, arrested them, and shot some on the spot. Haym was now a well-known member of the Sons of Liberty.

So soldiers rushed to his house and pounded on the door. "Open up! You're under arrest!"

The British marched Haym off to a jail called the Old Sugar House.

It was anything but sweet. A broken roof let in rain and soaked the prisoners. Cold and wet, Haym came down with a bad cough. He was moved to another jail, the Provost Prison. This one was even worse. Prisoners crowded the cell.

Hessian soldiers from Germany guarded them. The Hessians did not care about the American Revolution. They were career soldiers who fought other people's wars to earn money. The British had hired them to fight on their side and had brought them over to America.

Haym understood German, so he struck up a conversation. *"Guten Tag,"* he said to the guards. "Hello." When they gave him a piece of bread, he said, *"Danke schön.* Thank you."

The Hessian soldiers admired Haym's ability to speak different languages and told their commanding officer, General Heister, about him. General Heister realized that Haym could be useful as an interpreter. Haym could turn the Hessians' words into English, and he could translate the British general's orders into German. The British told Haym that the only way he could gain freedom was by working for the enemy. General Heister released Haym from jail on parole and gave him a job buying supplies for the

British prison. Haym agreed to help them but secretly vowed to use this opportunity to help other prisoners escape. And he did. As Haym worked with the Hessian guards, he became friends with them.

"Listen," he said, "why don't you run away? Pennsylvania is giving free land to any Hessian soldier who leaves the British army."

Many of the guards, especially the younger ones, took Haym's advice and deserted. General Heister had no idea what Haym was up to and rewarded him for his services by freeing him.

Haym opened a new office on Broad Street near City Hall.
Around this time, he met Rachel Franks, the daughter of a Jewish
merchant. They were married on July 6, 1777. The following
summer, their son, Ezekiel, was born.

Meanwhile, the war raged on. The American and British navies captured each other's cargo ships. Supplies were scarce. Nevertheless, Haym found a way to obtain and sell goods such as bread and rice. He kept working undercover with the Sons of Liberty. Haym helped more prisoners escape from the British jails and often hid them in his own house.

In August 1778, another fire broke out in New York, down at the docks. English ships burned. The Redcoats again blamed the Sons of Liberty. The next night, as Haym and Rachel finished dinner, they heard soldiers marching toward their house.

Someone pounded on the door. "Open—in the name of the king."

"Stay with the baby!" Haym shooed Rachel into the other room. He opened the front door.

"You're under arrest for treason," a Redcoat sergeant said. "You are a spy."

"Please let me say good-bye to my wife and baby," Haym said.

"Make it fast," said the sergeant.

Haym hurried into the bedroom, quickly hid some gold coins in his clothes, put on his jacket, grabbed his gold pocket watch, and kissed Rachel and their baby good-bye.

The Redcoats took Haym back to Provost Prison and threw him into a cell with twenty other men. Haym's fellow prisoners asked for news about the war. "Is General Washington winning?" "Will he ever recapture New York?" Haym told them what he knew. That night, he slept on the cold floor. His terrible cough came back. His chest hurt with every breath.

A few days later, the door to the cell opened and a guard led him away. Haym appeared before the prison warden and four British officers. They read the charges against him.

"Haym Salomon committed treason . . . He sheltered spies and gave them information . . . He plotted to burn the king's fleet of ships in the harbor of New York . . . He secretly communicated with General Washington . . ."

Some of the charges were true, others were false.

Finally the court allowed Haym to speak. "I admit that I tried to serve my country in whatever way I could," he said. The officers left the room to decide his fate. When they returned, one of them said, "We find the accused, Haym Salomon, guilty. We condemn the prisoner to be hanged by the neck until dead at dawn tomorrow."

Haym was taken back to jail and kept in a cell by himself. During the night, a young Hessian guard kept an eye on him. Haym spoke to him in German. He held out his watch and unwrapped the gold coins.

"I'll give you these if you leave my cell door open,"

he said. "Desert. Run north of New York to the Americans at Dobbs Ferry. I'll wait for an hour to give you a chance to get away."

The guard took the watch and coins. In the darkness, Haym heard a key turning in the lock. Holding his breath, he sat and waited. Then Haym tried the door. Open! He slipped down to the cellar, where the warden kept food for the prisoners. Finding the cellar doors, he slowly lifted one of them and felt the cool night air. Haym climbed up, then ran across the street into an alleyway. He was free!

Haym raced through the streets toward his house. As he approached, he saw British soldiers standing at his door. They were already searching for him. "I can't go home," Haym said to himself. "If I do, I'll put Rachel and the baby in danger."

So he turned and zigzagged through the streets, out of the city, past farms and fields, through forests. At last he reached Dobbs Ferry, where American troops were stationed.

Haym was shocked when he saw the condition of the poor soldiers. "You are dressed in rags," he said. "You don't even have uniforms."

"There is no money for uniforms," said the soldiers.

"We don't have enough to eat. And we are not getting paid, so we can't send money home to our families. How can we keep on fighting?"

Then and there, Haym formed a plan.

He went to the commanding officer, his old friend, General Alexander MacDougall. "Please give me a pass to go to Philadelphia," said Haym. "I can raise money to feed and clothe our troops." Haym knew that Philadelphia was the biggest and busiest city in all the colonies.

Alexander gave Haym a pass to show to American soldiers who might stop him along the way. For days and days, Haym walked—a distance of one hundred miles. He thought of his wife and baby. Would he ever see them again?

At last Haym arrived in Philadelphia. A religious man, he looked for a synagogue and found Congregation Mikveh Israel. Members of the congregation liked Haym and helped him get started in business again. He opened an office on Front Street near the busy docks. With his knowledge of foreign languages, he was able to talk to ship captains from different countries and trade with them. Representatives from France met with Haym in coffeehouses and arranged to loan him money for the American patriots. "We trust you," they said.

Haym's friends from Congregation Mikveh Israel helped Rachel and the baby come to Philadelphia.

Haym was overjoyed! His family settled into the house on Front Street where his office was located. Soon Haym and Rachel had two more children, daughters Sarah and Deborah.

Now Haym worked harder than ever before. "Business hardly gives me time to think what I am doing," he wrote to a friend. Haym worked so hard that his cough came back. Coughing spells hurt his throat and chest, so Rachel called for the doctor.

"Rest," the doctor ordered.

"I don't think I can rest," said Haym. "There is too much to do."

More and more people heard about Haym. One of them was Robert Morris, a Philadelphia businessman and patriot. Morris had been one of the signers of the Declaration of Independence in 1776. Now, in 1781, General Washington had appointed Morris as minister of finance. Washington gave Morris "the full power to raise the money needed to carry on the war." Morris invited Haym to meet at his house. On June 8, 1781, Morris wrote in his diary, "I agreed with Mr. Haym Salomon . . . to assist me." Haym became Morris's broker. He received loans or bills of exchange from France, Spain, and Holland to gain money for General Washington's troops. Usually he charged nothing for his services.

In the summer of 1781, Morris met with Washington at his headquarters north of New York. Washington needed money right away to lead a sneak attack against the British in Yorktown.

They agreed there was only one person who could do the job—Haym Salomon.

The story goes that on Yom Kippur, the Day of Atonement, Haym was attending services at Mikveh Israel. A messenger came in and asked for him.

"Robert Morris sent me," the messenger said to Haym. "He needs you to sell two bills of exchange for twenty thousand dollars."

Members of the congregation gasped. "For shame!" They were shocked to hear talk about money on the holiest day of the year for Jews.

Haym, however, knew that at no other time would he have so many people gathered at once. He asked the rabbi for permission to speak. "Let us all help General Washington," he said. Within a few minutes, Haym raised all the necessary money, including three thousand dollars of his own.

Thanks in part to Haym, Washington won the battle at Yorktown on October 19, 1781, and the British surrendered. The war was finally over. "Hurrah!" shouted Americans everywhere.

In the following years, the new American government led by George Washington still needed money. Haym helped establish a national bank, the Bank of North America, and continued working with Morris.

In 1784, Haym's health grew worse. His bad cough developed into a serious sickness, tuberculosis. On January 6, 1785, Haym died. He was forty-five years old. A few months later, his wife, Rachel, gave birth to their fourth child, a son named Haym Moses.

Haym Salomon left his family penniless. He had given away or loaned almost all he had for America. However, his efforts earned him an honorary place in history. Although Haym probably never met General George Washington, he stands beside him today in a statue. A bronze memorial in Chicago shows three American patriots clasping hands—Robert Morris, George Washington, and Haym Salomon.

AUTHOR'S NOTE

Little is known about Haym (pronounced *HIGH-im*) Salomon, the "Financier of the American Revolution." Only one portrait of him by an anonymous artist and a single sketch exist. Myths and legends have gathered about Salomon, a slender Jewish immigrant from Poland. The stories have held up because they are good, if not entirely true. Some historians believe that he may have been the first Jew of Polish birth to emigrate to America. Historians do agree about certain facts of his life according to records, letters, and diaries. Salomon wrote to the Continental Congress on August 25, 1778, reviewing his business and political activities. This book is based primarily on those sources. I particularly wish to thank Jonathan D. Sarna, professor of American Jewish History at Brandeis University and chief historian of the National Museum of American Jewish History, for his e-mail correspondence helping me to clarify fact from fiction. I have included some actual quotes from newspapers, diaries, and letters. Most of the dialogue and dramatic scenes, however, are my contribution to engage young readers in the story.

A portrait of Haym Salomon by an unknown artist

ARTIST'S NOTE

Library books were stacked on my desk and drawing tables for weeks in preparation for creating artwork for *Haym Salomon*. I wanted to learn as much as I could about the time period, clothing, even transportation. Here's an example: the point in the story where Haym's wife, Rachel, arrives in Philadelphia by boat. My rough sketch of Rachel walking off a humongous sailing ship was full of drama. I loved it. Seagulls were flapping all around. But Howard, my editor, reminded me that huge ships did not ferry people across the Delaware River! He suggested I draw her arriving by carriage. But doing research paid off—I found that during Haym Salomon's lifetime, they made the river crossing on flat-bottomed barges. So the dock scene got to stay in the book. It's much more dramatic to arrive by boat, even if it's a small one, don't you think?

If you'd like to learn more about how I make paintings, visit my Web site, www.davidslonim.com. See you there!

GLOSSARY

American Revolution—The war between the thirteen American colonies and England that lasted from 1775 until 1781, and resulted in a new nation, the United States of America.

bills of exchange—Written papers representing the amount of money a person or country borrows from a bank or a broker, and the date when the money is due to be paid back.

British—The people of Great Britain, also known as English.

broker—Someone who handles the loan of money from one person or country to another.

colonies—Lands in North America settled by many people from different countries but ruled by the British. They formed the original thirteen states of the United States of America.

colonists—People living in the thirteen colonies that originally belonged to England and then became the United States of America.

Declaration of Independence—A document written by a committee headed by Thomas Jefferson, and published on July 4, 1776, declaring that the United States of America were "free and independent."

desert—To run away from military service without planning to return.

exchange—To swap money from one country with an equal value of money from another country.

financier—A person skilled in managing large sums of money for others.

Hessian soldiers—Paid fighters who mostly came from the German state of Hesse-Cassel and were sent to fight in the American Revolution.

interpreter—Someone who explains the meaning of words spoken or written in a foreign language.

loans—Things or money that are borrowed for a certain length of time and expected to be returned.

minister of finance—A person appointed by a government to raise money for the country.

parole—The release of a prisoner from jail with certain conditions.

rebels—People who fight against the government or ruler of their country.

Redcoats—Another name for British royal troops, because they wore red jackets.

Sons of Liberty—An organized group of colonial rebels, whose members included John Adams, Samuel Adams, and Paul Revere, that fought for American independence.

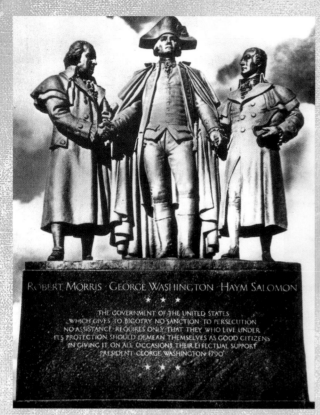

Robert Morris–George Washington–Haym Salomon Memorial, Chicago, 1941, by Lorado Taft

GLOSSARY (CONTINUED)

synagogue—A building for Jewish public prayer.

taxes—Sums of money that a government demands people pay for goods and services, such as schools and roadways.

trade—To buy and sell something for an amount of money, or to exchange items of equal worth.

translate—To change words from one language into another.

treason— A disloyal attempt to overthrow the government.

Yom Kippur—The Day of Atonement, the holiest day of the Jewish year.

END NOTES

"Army greatly distressed." Quoted in *New-York Gazette and the Weekly Mercury*, Monday, January 1, 1776.

"Many eat their shoes . . . we are *Americans* and *American Soldiers*." Quoted in *New-York Gazette and the Weekly Mercury*, Monday, January 15, 1776.

"Business hardly gives me time . . . what I am doing." Haym Salomon quoted in a postscript to a letter to Joseph Haines of Rockingham, August 31, 178—. From the Haym Salomon Collection, the American Jewish Historical Society, New York.

"the full power . . . carry on the war." George Washington, quoted in Rezneck, *Unrecognized Patriots: The Jews in the American Revolution*, as well as Laurens R. Schwartz, *Jews and the American Revolution: Haym Solomon and Others*.

"I agreed with Mr. Haym Salomon . . . to assist me." Robert Morris, quoted in his diary, in Harry Barnard, *This Great Triumvirate of Patriots*, p. 64.

BIBLIOGRAPHY

Books
* indicates books suitable for young readers

American National Biography, Volume 19, pp. 218–219. John A. Garraty and Mark C. Carnes, general editors. Oxford and New York: Oxford University Press, 1999.

*Amler, Jane Frances. *Haym Salomon: Patriot Banker of the American Revolution*. New York: Power Plus Books, 2004.

Barnard, Harry. *This Great Triumvirate of Patriots*. Chicago: Follett Publishing Company, 1971.

*Collier, Christopher, and James Lincoln Collier. *The American Revolution 1763–1783*. New York: Marshall Cavendish, Benchmark Books, 1998.

Dictionary of American Biography, Volume VIII, pp. 313–314 (entries *Platt* through *Seward*), edited by Dumas Malone. New York: Charles Scribner's Sons, 1935.

Fast, Howard. *Haym Salomon: Son of Liberty*. New York: Julian Messner, Inc., 1941.

Kitman, Marvin, Pfc. (Ret.) *George Washington's Expense Account*. New York: Grove Press, 1970.

*Langdon, William Chauncy. *Everyday Things in American Life: 1607–1776*. New York: Charles Scribner's Sons, 1937.

*Lukes, Bonnie L. *The American Revolution*. San Diego: Lucent Books, 1996.

Marcus, Jacob Rader. *Early American Jewry: The Jews of Pennsylvania and the South 1655–1790*. Philadelphia: The Jewish Publication Society of America, 1953.

*Marrin, Albert. *George Washington & the Founding of a Nation*. New York: Dutton Children's Books, 2001.

Randall, Willard Sterne. *George Washington*. New York: Henry Holt and Company, 1997.

Rezneck, Samuel. *Unrecognized Patriots: The Jews in the American Revolution*. Westport, Connecticut: Greenwood Press, 1975.

Schwartz, Laurens R. *Jews and the American Revolution: Haym Salomon and Others*. Jefferson, North Carolina, and London: McFarland & Company, Inc., Publishers, 1987.

Newspapers
The New-York Gazette and Weekly Mercury, January 23, 1775, to May 20, 1776. Worcester, Massachusetts: American Antiquarian Society, 1966.

Archival Collections
American Jewish Archives: The Jacob Rader Marcus Center, Cincinnati, Ohio. Web site: www.americanjewisharchives.org.

American Jewish Historical Society, New York, New York. Web site: www.ajhs.org.

Free Library of Philadelphia, Rare Book Department, Philadelphia, Pennsylvania.

To Edward Wolin, M.D., with gratitude
—S.G.R.

To my parents
—D.S.

Library of Congress Cataloging-in-Publication Data:

Rubin, Susan Goldman.

Haym Salomon : American patriot / by Susan Goldman Rubin ; illustrated by David Slonim.

p. cm.

ISBN 13: 978-0-8109-1087-4

ISBN 10: 0-8109-1087-X

1. Salomon, Haym, 1740–1785—Juvenile literature. 2. Revolutionaries—United States—Biography—Juvenile literature. 3. United States—History—Revolution, 1775–1783—Participation, Jewish—Juvenile literature. 4. Jews—United States—Biography—Juvenile literature. 5. Bankers—United States—Biography—Juvenile literature. I. Slonim, David, ill. II. Title.

E302.6.S17R79 2006

973.3092—dc22

[B]

2006013573

Book design by Celina Carvalho

Production manager: Alexis Mentor

Printed and bound in China

10 9 8 7 6 5 4 3 2 1

HNA
harry n. abrams, inc.
a subsidiary of La Martinière Groupe

115 West 18th Street

New York, NY 10011

www.hnabooks.com